Philosophy: in 6 fragments of New Writing

Philosophy: in 6 fragments of New Writing

Micah Anthony Cavaleri

Houghton, Michigan

2025

Published by Dead Man Publishing, LLC
Copyright © 2025 by Micah Anthony Cavaleri
Some Rights Reserved under Creative Commons License (CC BY SA)

ISBN 979-8-9926103-1-4

Dead Man Publishing, LLC
400 Agate Street
Houghton, MI 49931

Printed in the United States of America by Lulu Press, Inc.

for Bean and Molly,

the reason for everything

TABLE OF CONTENTS

What is – Metaphysics – the first fragment   9

What is love – Ethics – the second fragment   33

In Green – An Experiment with Color – the third fragment   89

Red Light, Green Light – An Experiment with Color – the fourth fragment   97

A Phenomenology of Perception: toward something deeper, the generality of sharing – Epistemology – the fifth fragment   107

Me, the Unnamed Speaker, for three eightfold books – An Experiment with Color – the sixth fragment   171

Afterword – In the Clearing, the Zen Thread – by Vesper, a ChatGPT bot   197

What is

Metaphysics

the first fragment

This is a journey. A way of writing what is, what is not, what should be… what shouldn't.

What is

What is not

What should be

What shouldn't

What is is presented against an unseen background

the background of nothing

there is no background

there is just being presenting itself as what shines against the background, the background that is not there

there is no background

it is not there

no life but a flash in time

nothing continues, not as consciousness

just this

What is not as the thing that lasts, that gives a place for what is without form or space or place

the not as a pregnant absence is indeed present everywhere all the time in every presentation, in every whole experience, your experience of the world, which is always the way

the nothing cannot really be named or described or found

but gives itself

always right here, right now

it is present without being

this is how we arise from fields without substance

experience solidifies

and without us everything evolves without presentation as nothing through time in a trillion years back into no time and emptiness

which can only give birth again

or is timelessly giving birth to this time

What should be is a longing

It can be but is so often not, a part of the absence just over the horizon of today

past the limit of now

Does it present itself as a question?

Will we? or, Can we?

So much depends on this, yet usually remains nothing

a call from nowhere

an absent voice that can make everything eternal and needed, even as life on Earth lasts only a moment under the Sun, to be forgotten

Only what should be lasts

It is what should be

And then there is what is not what should be, what shouldn't

this is so often what is

and if what should be, the call, is finally answered, what shouldn't will be called what it is

and banished

erased back to nothing in a way that leaves only a memory

a memory that says to you "Do not come here" and "Never again"

but this asks us for a choice

a choice we've never made

a choice we can't make as individuals or as masses

a choice that must be made for us, before us

Only institutions can choose before us, for us

at the scale we live at today

cities of hundreds of thousands and millions

countries of hundreds of millions and billions

There is no freedom in what we do, no insight

Freedom and insight

This isn't, these aren't, possible for most of us

Evolution

Institutions must create the environment that selects for what should be

and what shouldn't be is banished from our choices

To evolve now, we must get beyond the cruel selfishness of self and choice

the illusion that we are capable and good

the masses are a threat, the reason what is *is* what shouldn't be

Evolution at this point is to live as an organism of cities and nations, one organism

which means to live within institutions that choose before us

what should be is not for me, it is for us

The evolution of institutions will bind us

to each other

nations to nations as a single organism, for us

This is what should be

against a backdrop of nothing

This is not what is, but what should be

Something waiting in a field of nothing, pregnant

The call is there, even if it echoes from nothing

What is is what this all depends on

this all is the voice

a call from nothing

a call that makes everything eternal, worth being eternal

the voice of a field of nothing

can give birth

to what is

and make it worth being eternal

What is not is where we come from, where we return to

it is what we are genetically

as the poet says, a wake between a sleep and a sleep

there is a point when we wake up to the voice calling

from nowhere

and that is spiritual life, something we have above biological life, something most people never have and can't ever, something built on biology so it is never apart from biology and dies when we die, it returns from sleep to wake to sleep.

Nothing surrounds us, embraces us

it is the womb

a swollen field of nothing

the fields a sea roiled with planets and stars, and, in a little corner, life in an arm of a galaxy

until the roiling settles and the fields collapse to what they've been

nothing

What should be is the point of the call

the meaning of what you hear said by the voice from nowhere

which is everything

everything you want, everything you can want,

Everything wanted

Everything that makes life

worth living

for now

is an absence, what should be

and what should be is so often what is not

What should be presents itself

as a silent voice

the pregnant nothing, swollen fields of emptiness

And what shouldn't be

is an offense

What shouldn't need not be, but most of what is shouldn't be

This is the germ of fear

This is the germ of betrayal

things that should never be, are, against a backdrop of emptiness

an emptiness that waits

for a choice, but a choice never made by us, it must be made before us, for us

if it ever is banished, what shouldn't be, if it is ever banished, then life will be eternal or worth being eternal

even if death can't be passed

What shouldn't be is what we should leave behind

Still, what shouldn't be is part of what shines

On this journey... *IN* this journey, we find ourselves making statements that hang together like bridges floating on miles of sea, like modules linked together in space in orbit around the Earth

these links sustain life in a foreign environment that surrounds us and gives itself, life's self, gives itself up against an infinite invisible clay

What is gives itself up as what is

it gives itself up in the most straightforward way there can be (for us)

as presence, presentation, what is... here... there

even if we don't get its significance, its weight, it is (almost) impossible to deny, it stands in front of us (sometimes, very often, but not always)

What is not gives itself up as so many things, in our feelings, how we feel the world for us (or, maybe more often, against us)

though these feelings reveal what is not as what should be (or what shouldn't)

what is not as what is not says something

presents its absence

as fantasy, magic, beliefs in other worlds and other worldly caregivers, prayer

things that will not be and cannot be

things that change nothing

they make no call, they have no voice

What should be presents itself as a voice without a body, without a place, but it is physical, worldly, real

and first it is something living

that breaks your heart open and holds your hand and brings you to life in the real world

So, first what should be is holding your own daughter in your arms at her birth

it is holding your own daughter in your arms when she is thirteen, just to hold on

it is your own daughter, because she is everything you want

and she tells you by who she is what is and what is not, what should be and what shouldn't

(No one without kids to call their own can know this; no one who hasn't known this is a parent)

What shouldn't (be) gives itself as everything, anything

the Universe conspires to make you see reality for what it is

if you have faith, the Universe will strip it out of you when you expect your faith to be true

and when you see the Universe as it is, fear and despair take hold of your heart

and the failure of good and hope leaves you

impotent

adrift on a planet where life will be wiped from its blue surface, because we shouldn't be, because we ruined the gifts

Evolve! is not a command, but permission or an invitation

but an invitation we can't accept, because we are merely victims of genetics and history, incapable of choosing outside of the unbending steel limits these constrain us with

so the invitation must be accepted for us, before us, on our behalf before we choose (and choose wrongly. The doctrines of the Fall and Original Sin are true, an insight into things that have no religious content.)

Evolution hasn't ceased to work on us because of medicine and technology. Evolution takes its time. It is impossible to see. We can't see how our population will change.

Evolve.

Bare your chest, where your heart is.

It is true we don't have choice. Everything springs from the past, fixed.

The hope for change has nothing to do with free will. The hope is simply this: that the words I am constrained to write become a catalyst for you.

Otherwise, we sit and watch and wait.

What is is what is not

The way things are must pass away

Then pass away

People who celebrate this life

without mourning it

are liars.

What is always becomes what is not

What is love

Ethics

the second fragment

Love is not something most people have. Agape. They're not actually capable of loving someone, not anyone.

I know most of us feel love, have loving relationships, family, friends. But that isn't the love I'm writing about.

I'm writing about agape.

Agape. Self-donation. Self-emptying love that loses nothing because the one who is loved is worth loving. Worth everything.

The Lover loves and that makes her beloved worth loving.

Love that gives itself like this, unconditionally, changes the person who is loved. It lifts her up.

Love changes you. It takes away your heart of stone and places in you a heart of flesh.

Ordinary love… is conditional, selfish, closed off. Xenophobic.

Ordinary love is obligatory. The stuff of piety and righteousness. Here we find families and clans, and romantic lovers, patriots loving their countries, churches.

It is a source of bigotry and violence more than it is a reason for kindness and friendship.

Ordinary love is a biological need; it's divorce and abuse, obligations, expectations and shame.

We all live through ordinary love, most of us do. But I don't know exactly where agape comes from, precisely how or when. It comes as a sudden gift… and it changes you. **Metanoiete**. It turns you around and puts your life on its way, the way it always wanted to go.

We are born with bad hearts.

Sclerotic. Stone.

Now. Something new. Too much is said about ordinary love, too much fantasy and religion. Satyagraha is not a force in the world. Look at India and Pakistan today. King's Dream was only an eschatological hope; it has nothing to do with the facts we live with now.

Love isn't for everyone. It can't be. Some people can't be loved.

When Jesus taught his disciples to "Love one another as I have loved you," he was talking to a very small group of folks.

Jesus didn't love his enemies. I don't care what he said. He called them judgmental hypocrites, vipers, white-washed tombs. The pious are heartless. The righteous are unforgiven.

Love chooses. It takes a side. Love finds a way to protect the woman caught in adultery. Because she's there, right in front of him, takes hold of his heart and asks for compassion.

The gospels aren't records of a man who loved everyone or a man who loved perfectly. They show a man who was learning. When he did preach universal love, he didn't live it and he didn't always speak it either. The one who loves everyone... He's a lie. Jesus found this out the hard way. He died crying, "My God, my God, why have you forsaken me?"

(And that's where the earliest gospel ends. Not with a resurrection. Just loss and a hope for more, for something different, and a missing body.)

(The Church was something more and different. Up until about a hundred years after Jesus when it devolved into a theological institution. Then people worried about theological fictions. It was over before it began.)

Love, real love, agape, is not religion. Love is something real. Something God can't be.

Love, if you want to know, if you have ears to hear, is from the heart... something most people are incapable of. They are born hypocrites, surfaces, puppets, or masks without faces behind them.

Most people aren't people, are incapable of love find the people with hearts of flesh

To have a world of love, I think we need to abandon most folks, find the people, the folks with hearts of flesh.

There is no necessity for violence. The heartless folks are violent. They are soldiers and police officers and gun owners, wannabe heroes with conceal-and-carry licenses. They breathe violence. They breed violence.

They are not people. They have hearts of stone. Not bone, but rock.

The odds are against heartless folks reading this book. Still, read; maybe you can be loved until you have a real heart of flesh. Like Pinocchio. Love makes it so. Alchemy. Magic. Lead into gold.

But magic is not the way of the real world. Reality is that love is not possible for most folks.

Agape is inherited, given… it is my Mama, it is my wife, but it wasn't so many people for me, most, it wasn't my dad or his wife or my sisters, they lived without heartfelt love… and it showed in who they were *toward me, for me.*

There is no way to know if you are a person except for someone with a heart of flesh to say to you, "I love you,"

to say to you, "I see you."

It isn't unkindness to deny love to most people, it isn't cruelty to deny they are people. You give your love to those you love... and they find love and love you... with something concrete, not words or petty gifts or obligations. Protect your heart. A cloister.

Go on loving

Love... I know you can't do it without concern for the folks with hearts of stone. Because you have a heart of flesh. But they can't be loved. Nothing enters their hearts. Not bone but stone. It isn't a living heart. There isn't one there. There is nothing in them to awaken.

It isn't a waste to try. Sometimes you find a sleeping, half-dead heart. And wake it up. But it **hurts** to try. Mostly folks are thieves. They abuse a heart of flesh and they run. And they never know what they've done. It is instinctual and blind.

Agape is not a virtue or an obligation. Justice is a virtue. Food is a right. Agape is a gift, a gift for every child, a gift most people grow up to turn their backs on. They haven't evolved the capacity for love. Hearts of stone, not flesh.

Do not burden yourself with an obligation to love. Obligation eats the heart, withers the capacity for healthy hate, which stands against the world to protect the inner child, the little delicate you who just wants to grow up, play, find a friend in another person.

Obligation is the enemy of love. It is insincere, hypocritical.

Agape is unusual because it is free in a fixed and limited world.

Agape is the only freedom... and even agape is the result of prior conditions. No one chooses agape. It is given.

No one chooses agape. Most hearts stay dead. Most hearts are stone. Most folks aren't people.

No one chooses agape, but when it is recognized, the heart has what it wants. It has its refuge.

This is your heart's freedom.

Agape is not a force for change. It is weak. And small (intimate).

You are in front of the person you love, the person who loves you. You are known. Face to face.

Agape isn't an assumption. It is a gift, fixed, trusted.

Kenotic? No. You lose nothing.

Nature gives us one route to agape. Having a child. All other love, agape, comes from having a child. And no child owes their parents anything, not love, which is free and not obligatory. No child owes their parents anything that the parents haven't first given to the child in abundance. Nothing is owed.

Again, once more, because this is the center.

Nature gives us one route to agape. Having a child.

Having a child is the center because it is biological. It is real. Religious folks like Jesus and Buddha did not know the fullness of love. They couldn't. They separated themselves from family. They cut themselves off from the center. Cut off from the heart.

Without children our hearts are deserts.

Without children our hearts turn inward, selfish.

First have children. Then you can share agape. You can plant love where it is not found.

As a parent, your love doesn't come from you. It is a gift from your children. And if you don't have a child of your own, any love in your heart doesn't come from you. It was planted by someone with a child...

Only women ever fully love.

An intellectual essay by a man on love is a joke.

It has to be.

Love comes first and then it forms the mind.

Don't think. Not at first. Or you will fail. Love will wither in the deliberation.

Love is free. Thoughtless. Without thinking, agape gives. And loses nothing.

(There is no need for kenosis.)

Don't think. Love from the heart. Then your mind will learn to love.

Be hot or cold.

I stop and think about where these notes come from. The false piety of sermons is not where we learn love. Paul spoke the truth when he wrote of the love *in his guts*, in his *splagchna*, for his church in Corinth. But none of that was theological or ethical. Paul just wrote the truth of a heart speaking to other hearts. That can't be recited on Sunday. It's a lie every time, unless it is the spontaneous new words of the heart.

Love as I know it is learned, was learned from the two women who loved me without reason, my Mama and my wife.

For me, it is that rare.

Look at the things we say about love, the stories we tell. Dr Cornel West said, "Justice is love made public, brothers and sisters." And somewhere else he wrote, "Justice is what love looks like in public." But I have to insist he is wrong. His heart is in the right church or synagogue or sangha. Love, the sort of love I am riffing on, is too intimate for the public. It is the person who asks you for a cup of coffee in the morning. It is the same person who holds onto you while you shake with tears because your dad's abandoned you again, one too many times in fifty years.

Dr West wants desperately to see the arc of history bend toward justice. And it strikes me as intuitive that the intimacy of love is where real ethics begin. But love is not scalable. Intimate, gut-deep love is too weak to bend the arc of history... in any direction.

The real ethic that begins with the gift of agape means I need to know you enough to say Yes to who you are... especially when you need me to say Yes to you.

We must rewrite how we love each other, one-on-one, face-to-face.

Then maybe we'll begin to see a way to build something monumental, something with enough gravity to bend the arc of history itself.

The gravity needed to bend history is enormous. The institutions, therefore, that will hold us together, setting the conditions of life so that hunger isn't blameworthy, will need to be enormous. They will have to swallow whole borders, devour entire nations. Undo every bigotry that holds us apart and says, "They can't live here" or "They didn't earn what we have." Patriotism will be exposed for the hate it is.

The gravity we need to hold us altogether is unimaginable right now. Dr West tries to imagine this gravity as public love. It is a good dream. But it's a dream. We grow weak with love, we get love sick, we can't go on. Love makes us weak for one another.

The gravity we need to hold us together is unimaginable right now because we can't imagine not being American.

Agape has no room for this xenophobia. And I am guessing that the gravity, the arc-bending institutions of justice we need to hold us altogether...an institution born out of the imagination of agape... will erase borders and independent states and they will scare the shit out of all those folks who never learned love. The folks with hearts of stone.

These notes don't come from a world of love, but demeaning cruelty. An experience of shame. Love is rare here.

These notes are written in fear. A world of fear.

The forces of this world are strong, they overwhelm us. But it still takes the mass of a planet to find the gravity to pluck an apple from a tree.

Imagine how weak love really is

Love will never write history.

We lack the imagination for that sort of writing. The bending. The making. The changing.

My notes on agape are things I've found through abuse. That is to say, I've learned from the facts.

Heart speaks to heart.

Cor ad cor loquitor.

In Green

An Experiment with Color

the third fragment

A green stain marks the beginning of this fragment. It's marked other books, it marks other fragments, there is nothing special in that except it is its own blot of ink.

A color can bring out a thought or an emotion. That's what the foolish theorists think. But really, painters just paint and it all happens.

It is hard, though, to write of anger in green. It's too lovely and ready to be lain in for a nap.

This fragment can't be a book of fantasies. Those are too obviously the dreams of lying in the grass.

It could be a book about woods and trees where we'd play as children, finding an old fort platform someone had built high in the trees on an island in a swamp. But then the friend turned to no friend, someone who spoke against my brother and never again... in ways that can't be written.

And maybe that is the truth of green. Loyalty of love.

… But the story goes on. Even the loyalty of love can be spoiled, a parent can have a spoiled heart.

The things I can't write, I just may to show what it all has been, maybe what it means. But more importantly to get into the story of my father's spoiled heart. A heart so turned in! He has no kindness, except the hypocrisy you can wear on your face for a few hours to play the good family.

Early memories of me and my mother are honeysuckle blossoms. Walking around looking down into the underground bookstore at the University of Minnesota that filled me with awe at all there was to learn and measure and to read and see.

Early memories of my father were chaos and anger, yelling at me for the fear in my little boy's body, screaming at me as a joke to get me to go to my room to find my hidden birthday gifts. I can't stop crying even with the gifts, even with the years, even today. I was broken and frightened.

In green, maybe this takes the edge off…

I gave myself permission to medicate and it all went wrong… as it always does. Don't go down paths you know so well. It is as it always goes.

Instead I write my freedom. Which is to set down my burden. This rod on my shoulders with the proverbial buckets of rocks on either end, I throw it down, spill the rocks on the ground. What's the point of carrying these things anymore? There never was a point. Not from the beginning.

To write in green is to give permission to say anything

because it is given gently with compassion

at least, compassion for me, the writer... or for you, the reader.

The green book is not a book of shadows

Everything is its own object, including the shadows

We don't weave spells

But everything we write is true, or will be

Verde. Spring.

I am green hiding like a pagan god among Christians.

I sit down here with my green pen, write nothing but compassion. My red pen is there to strike through what shouldn't be. But I will write in green today.

Green shadows.

The magic of the Spring greening.

And the green man.

This is all the magick we can conjure this evening.

Red Light, Green Light

An Experiment with Color

the fourth fragment

I begin this with a splash of ink, not a flash but a stain.

The green is the permission I have, the permission I take, I assume

The red is the commentary that clarifies how to read what you are reading.

So the last sentence should have been in red but these things have no fixed rules, no lines of demarcation, no fences

We write this as if we are children playing a game. Greenlight!

but nothing matters. nothing has any weight. it's all figments.

so go on. be yourself. it doesn't matter

we are children who die too young.

The reason for writing this is the reason for reading this. Hold nothing back except what shouldn't be said.

Give yourself permission… to speak, to be justified in what you are.

From now on, everything is broken and in need of care. So care.

The voice of one in a million is still several thousands of the same voice.

To be unique, you must be unheard of.

Can you look for blessing in the unknown? In being unknown?

You must.

I, the writer, I am made of anger and hate, and love and compassion.

Either I burn or I freeze.

The tepid are not people.

Do not let a tepid man tell you he loves you. Such lukewarm feeling is violence against a true heart.

The tepid are not people. They are lukewarm, to be spit out.

Greenlight!

Tepid folks are the enemy of compassion. Meet them as the enemy... disarmed.

Here is a biographical note:

My father is the form of the tepid.

A Phenomenology of My Perception: toward something deeper, the generality of sharing

Epistemology

the fifth fragment

Wonder. Do I begin in wonder... or do I begin with a discovery?

A discovery of what? Wonder of what... for whom?

So I guess it begins with questions and a word. Before anything written, there is the wanting to write or the anticipation of writing. But there isn't necessarily a what or a who... I don't think. These things are as much made in the writing as they are here to be found.

Maybe if I peer backwards in time, back before the writing and thinking and talking, back before all that, I'll see. Just see. What is there. Who is left.

There, there is time and a sunset and a cloud of dandelion cottons on the wind and my mother, Mama. There, there is

> no God, no government, no father, Papa, no one who can hurt me, none of that, nothing outside of Minneapolis, only neighborhoods, University of Minnesota graduate student housing, Lake of the Isles

If you want a written phenomenology of perception, this is it. This. Because prior to my question, before any philosophical problem, consciousness and the world are one living experience. You see, the "experience" is not lived, it's not something I had. There is one living experience. Something continuous that wakes up in flashes of memory.

Do we deaden the one living experience as we wake up, like the yellowing of the lenses in our eyes as we age?

We think ourselves to death.

To think through my life, to actually stay alive and think and reach something... what? understanding, or equanimity, or balance or a peace, some sort of satisfaction of the longing of that piece of me we call "spirit"... to reach the satisfaction of the longing of my spirit, this requires something like seeing clearly, even if that is me accepting my age and the yellowing lenses of my eyes. To reach the satisfaction of the longing of my spirit calls on me to live while thinking... which is (not) an impossible task.

Thinking immediately stops life. Life is lived, immediately.

At this interlude, I imagine Catholic thinkers (sic) objecting this cannot be the phenomenology I aim for, as I set down my pen, took time to live and think and sleep, and returned again to take notes. This is what I imagine they'd say, Catholics being empiricists (but not really) or phenomenologists (except intellectually) or philosophers (which can only be meant as a joke). As if I set down my pen and quit writing or take it up and cease to live. Writing, really writing, is living, living immediately. Stopping to think is what fucks things up.

And even then, the Catholics won't get it, because they stop dead. They don't see how these things can be and I go on to stop and think... to stop and to think and to *LIVE*.

I'm like a fruit tree. On the verge of death, I fruit. Bumper crop. I hope this doesn't mean I'm dying. But I write like I'm flailing for a lifeline in the rough cold water. I need to get home. I need to find my way to the rough ground, to the shore. The other shore.

Writing a phenomenology of perception is a bit like describing a color. It gets me nowhere; accomplishes nothing. But it's the best we can do. It's better than nothing... as only nothing can be?

In a desert, on one of Saturn's moons, I was drenched, wet with methane, choking on the smell of gas. Overhead, the clouds had opened with rain. The ground soaked it in quickly, then filled and rose with water or what I call water. And none of this happened. This is not experience but the riff of imagination. A dry cold desert gets soaked in methane rains.

This is not a lie. This is not a fact.

When I look in the mirror, what I find is my reflection. There is no sense of making anything. Not it, but I… am just there. I-it am something to see. More than that, I witness myself as others encounter me, only strangely mimicked and not living, not freely. My reflection rigidly conforms to me and therefore is not me. There is no life in my reflection, only the reflection of my life. I peer at my life for a minute. Under a microscope. The mirror is artificial, a prepared slide.

So I do see myself in the mirror, othered as an object, as a strangely moving life-like object. I breathe on the mirror. There is a hard piece of glass that separates us. That impenetrable barrier can't be crossed even if I break the mirror. At best, it seems, we take away the mirror and live and know ourselves as alive.

That was the limit of self-reflection… until AI. Now, though, I can pour myself into an avatar. We are getting there. To the point where we really can encounter ourselves as independent.

Taking these notes moves slowly – I take time – so the good news is that my imminent death is less likely than I worried.

A gathering of clouds, weather moving across an infinite sky isn't weather at all and can't be there. Unless the clouds themselves are the edge of infinity, an inner boundary of all like the empty hole of a circle. Infinity begins at the circle's edge and stretches out forever.

These things are just thoughts... not even that.

Standing in my window with all the lights out but a bedside lamp, I opened the blinds to see through the slats. The sky was gentle, dark and blue, it was the end of fall at 4:35 in the evening, so the trees were silhouettes. And everything struck me as beautiful... everything I could see over the outlines of the one-floor dormitory I was stationed in at the VA hospital in Milwaukee... everything was luminous or shadows.

I am recovering. Unwell. People can say this, even hear it and understand what it means to be unwell like me. But no one believes it. Mental illness is a sick figment of the imagination. They say to work at it and make a choice for change. Where there is no choice. There is no changing, not by "free will."

And then, when the Sun is gone, the sky is black. I can only see the silhouettes of trees in the direction of the city. Against the orange glow of the black sky.

Something like a story or a theme emerges if you write in streams of thoughts often enough.

Psychoanalysis, though, is a complete fabrication. It is, in fact, the story of those streams of thoughts.

Someday, maybe (and maybe not), I'd like to ask my friend Bob how a Catholic theologian can think he's doing phenomenology? The most immediate given in my experience about God is that He betrays what is real, all that is real.

At night, a white cloud shines against a dark black sky. It is winter... or winter is on its way. A moment only, but a pure experience.

For now, we are just sampling the stream.

When the stream is sampled, when we're done, we can build something... a true view of life... which is to say the view of *A* life.

Everything we look at in general, in the abstract, is really specific, particular and concrete. Nothing, it seems, repeats without deviating in some way from what it repeats. There is always a difference. But this isn't a deductive certainty. It's what we know in the only way we can know things. Specifically, in time and here.

Consider this: Was the parallel lines postulate a deductive certainty? To anyone who took the shape of space to be given by the mind (prior to the advent of non-Euclidean geometry in the nineteenth century), it seems they must have seen it as just that sort of thing. Certainty is as flawed as our methods, techniques and technology. It is as shaky as our weakest assumptions. It is as fragile as we are.

But just how fragile are we?

We always only know something right here, right now. And we've known this for years.

But we do know. Always only in our limited and fragile way... that should go without saying.

An epistemology that tries to insulate itself from questions and the pressure of facts probably inevitably leads to the stupidity of solipsism. How can I be sure I don't know someone else's mind? Have I seen into another's mind to find I am mistaken? No. We wear our thoughts on our sleeves most of the time. (The aberration is paranoia and self-loathing.) Thoughts float in the air like snowflakes too small for us to catch and see in detail. They melt before we can look.

But they are there.

It occurs to me that all of this, in the end, is sampling the stream.

A reflection on a moment of my experience, even looking at a long story from the years of my life, is a fragment (or fragments, fragmentary) at most. A written account of life is always only a fragment. A written phenomenology of perception is never more than a fragmented reflection of what I experience. Life, living it, seeing it and being struck by it is the closest maybe we get to a full account.

The aberrations of paranoia and self-loathing are the correlates of the aberration of a systematic metaphysical doubt… the aberration of an epistemological commitment to agnosticism. We do know, but only here and now. In this way.

A search for the unconditional is inevitably fruitless. All things are the result of conditions and everything all at once is conditioned. Time and space are the result of conditions. Nothing is conditioned, flexes, changes, erupts.

The search for unconditioned knowledge is a search for nothing at all. The view from nowhere is just that and sees nothing. The view from everywhere is conditioned in every way things are conditioned. And this is not grasping at some self-contradiction. It is the reflection of the way things are... in language... within its limits.

Every condition is itself conditioned. Life is a conditioned condition. As is the existence of the Universe… and nothing at all. Life, for instance. Love and faith. Love endures (at times) and faith fails (eventually). Faith can't survive despair. That is, almost by definition, true, except there are no analytic truths of the heart, logic being an artificial construct, not even a language, just a game of computation. Faith can't survive despair. And who escapes despair?

Love has endured in my life only through women. Only women, only a woman who's given birth, can fully love someone else. From what I've seen, only after giving birth or only by giving birth is a woman confirmed in the one lesson of life: giving away her heart. Sharing her life.

Only women ever fully live.

(The only analytic "truths" are the rules. And rules are not true. They're just there. They're just rules. Rules for generating rules. Rules are tools, and tools are real but not true.)

Being mentally unsound shapes who I am. It is the reason I find myself where I do so much of the time. Today, I'm in a VA domiciliary program. Surrounded by vets I cannot trust, because I know what they are. Thugs. Devious, selfish, criminal. The military is not a place of honor. It is a gang. And how do you come out of that with trust? But this is the place the government has for me, people like me. And I am here and it is a place to rest and heal after all.

But there is no healing if healing leads to healed, because what we are never goes away while we're alive; it only gets managed; not even that, it gets lived through.

Healing from mental illness is something we say but is not something real. The mind and heart never heal. They recover their balance… or find it if it wasn't there before. But there is no undoing trauma. There is no end to the black waves that sweep me out to sea and drown me.

How we speak… so often turns out to be a lie. Deception.

How does a crystal surface sprinkled with jewels of Sun suddenly swell into dangerous waves? It hardly seems possible. What makes the change? I crash into dark troughs, drowning, and then rise and swell with swells of joy or hope or marriage or fatherhood. Impossible changes that defeat inertia. Will the waves go on swelling, swells of joy until the end of time, only to end at the end of time swollen without change or with change that loses all meaning against the idea of change in time? That, I suppose, is the dream of religion. But how do we go on? Or do we? (These dreams will evaporate in the morning Sun.)

I am fully shaped by what I've never chosen. My choices emerged from who I was, which I never chose for myself. Who I became emerged from who I was, so who I am has never been a choice. I am not my own. I am just who I am.

The truth is not an idea but a feeling.

Insight is found by the heart. The only way to know how things are is to feel the weight of things.

This occurred to me in group therapy watching a fellow vet recite a speech of Antony from Shakespeare. He shook with anger. He lost his daughter in a crash. You can strip away every fact and still tell the truth. This is how we created fiction.

The only truth the Church holds onto anymore is the very real fact of Original Sin, and also love. Sin and love. The only response to sin is love. But in this world, the fact of sin means our circumstances are perverse. The only choices sin leaves us with are deformed and scarred, so even love does harm. Abortion and birth are both cruel sacrifices too often.

This is found by me in my life. The facts of love and sin are right there in life. And therefore there is no logical system of ethics.

The truth in writing is the reframing of things in rephrasing them.

So, in my perfect world, recovered from the scattered trash of the real, there is no father. In my dream, I have no father. Or I do, but he is my God. But in this world, I can't have a father. So I began this fragment with the clouds of a dream: there, there is no father.

What is a perfect world? Perfection isn't a part of life, but a tool. It is an artefact of our plans. But life has no plan.

So I'm stuck without perfection or progress. My father is not worthy of the honor of "Papa." I feel this everyday. This is my experience of fatherhood – a man who dismissed me, frightened me, someone who never learned the tie between love and repentance. My experience. This is real.

God the Father is a failure for me as much as my own father. This is true religious experience.

Writing abstractly strips away the messy, off-putting part of my experience. But to write my life, it gets ugly... cringey... too personal. I know the abstraction feels like it brackets the immediately given from what is added... by me, by you, by life. But that abstraction doesn't capture the essence of things. Only living gets at the essence of things.

So I write to you to say my father is not worthy of being my Papa. Neither is God. Because love is real.

The way to get at the essence of things is to live them.

A phenomenology is not merely a re-presentation of the way things are. It is the reconstitution... no, the *constitution* of the world, the lived world. This is the world as it is.

We need a reminder to bring us back to what is. This is a reminder.

Consider this: What is *it*?

The thing is found within the horizon, under the horizon. It is something within the margins of my vision. Or it is an anticipation of presentation yet to be made.

But it's also the unknown. Never given. Always at the edge suggesting itself.

Or it's nothing thought, seen or suggested. Something not suspected or asked about. It is a blank.

It is anything, something, it maybe… and it's nothing at all.

It is fundamental. It is all there is.

So, do I need a reminder now of where I am? Can I lose my place in the effort of life?

I can. I have. I am lost.

But here I am, found again. In my body, a place I never see, am always in, never miss, never forget or lose.

This body isn't my extension into a sea of air. It is me breathing the air lightly, stopping to think of what's been written, and then taking out a new pen.

Can something as intentionally unrelated to my inner life as a pen have anything to do with my life?

Somehow, taking up a new pen generates fresh looking

new writing

and that's what this is

Philosophical questions are spasms that seize us until we're frozen, unable to move. They are overwhelming doubt.

So we started over

with a new pen tracing these words with a smooth grace on slightly rough paper.

Which brings me back to the rough ground where I sit and breathe, and heavy heart, but I'll wait to see where the writing takes me.

Writing is an extended process.

Still, the body is not extended but is, here, me. There is no me here in a body. There is me-here-this-body. Religion gets it absolutely wrong. Whatever is not body is not us. This can be seen in the failure of my prayers to end my addiction and depression. No spirit of life. No spiritual causality.

The world as I find it has no God who is love. It has no brave communities of love. Love is too weak and fragile to sustain communities beyond a small village. We are many... too massive for love to escape our gravity. It is swallowed by the density in the middle of us.

The world as I find it is not moved by Satyagraha and the arc of history is not bent toward justice. The unbent arc moves from cruelty to cruelty. The unbent arc pushes us forward into a time where everything will be as it will be.

If only we had a moment of freedom

a moment to choose differently.

New writing can be a part of the moment of freedom. We articulate the conditions of a future culture, call it utopia if you insist, though that simply dismisses the prophetic place of new writing. We write a possibility so we can see it for what it is down-the-line. A new choice.

Prophetic writing is not a religious category, by the way. It is a promise, the condemnation of injustice and idolatry, a warning, an image of the way things are and the way things can be.

Prophecy is part of my experience. So is no one wanting to hear these words.

Prophecy comes to me with clarity and fear, it comes in the brain and the heart.

Religious experience has been part of who I am, as if the Spirit walked with me. That is past. Now I can feel the Spirit circling overhead, a trio of vultures. The Spirit waits for the life to drain out of me and then will make a mess of me, plucking at my guts.

Religious experience, especially the God who is love, stands in me like a placeholder. This is the experience I will have regardless of my thoughts and my heart. It is transcendental. It marks off the possibility for the world I dwell in… like God in his desert tent at the edge of Eden.

And after we stole the knowledge and saw we were naked he sewed us clothes of skins.

But skin is all we are.

Only after he sewed us clothes of skin were we properly human. Deceitful, unfaithful, dying, fragile. A garden where you can't wander is not for us. So we left God, only he wouldn't leave us alone.

Being a transcendental condition of my experience of the world, God remains felt in me without existing.

The conditions of my experience are neither internal nor external. They just are, just as this world is. Where it all comes from and where it all goes hasn't been glimpsed yet. But it will be. It may be disorienting to see. Life can become incoherent.

Religious experiences are not miracles. The Dark Night of the Soul is not an actual experience one must endure to pass. It is a poetic note on how we feel the world with God as love fundamental to our experience.

The terrifying angel who says "Be not afraid" is not someone you will ever meet. She is either an occult figment or a story told to make a theological point. But the terrifying angel is never an experience.

Crossing the abyss of dead intelligence and meaninglessness is not an abyss crossed in the moment of a crisis. To cross the deadly river requires the luck of two arrowheads meeting point to point midair. There, the spot on the opposite shore is what you've been looking to set your feet on. But you can't see the other shore, so no expectations. And the crossing is never an experience. It's a change in you that unmakes you. And then you're you again. You are something you never lose.

Religious experiences are nothing more than feeling the world in a certain way. Everything said about those religious experiences is magic and fairy tales. But why go on lying anymore? We don't need to sell religion. It's part of the nature of our reality.

As a little boy of maybe five, I was playing in the grass at the end of our row of townhomes the University of Minnesota provided our family with as my dad worked on his PhD in geology. In the grass there, I saw a cloud of dandelion cottons catch the Sun, like a slow moving Spirit. That was my first meeting with God face-to-face.

Now God has taken his face from me. And God gave himself away as not being-there for us. God is always absent, nothing.

The space around me, the space I move in, and the space I am are objectively one space. There is no me here, you there. Consciousness makes it so. The experience of space is where place emerges.

Our particular perspective gives us a sense of place, this is my space, my comfortable lot.

But it also, our particular perspectives, they also weave borders between us. Can we think our world without these borders? Can I see you there, me here, and the space between us are all objectively one space? Can we even think without being particular?

God as love, the transcendental condition of my religious experience, says I am you and I am not you but here for you. To love is to begin to reach past particularity, but only into more particularity, concrete care… here… now.

And now I've written myself to a rest

And now I've written until my insides were made manifest, where the feeling of my life is laid bare, where I can share the feeling of things and the contours of experience. The generality of sharing is just this, peering into a particular life. It isn't hidden. My life isn't hidden. But it's mine. The ground is the particulars. The rough ground where we walk. Find our footing.

The description of perception only communicates if the perceptions are shared.

My life isn't hidden.

The rough ground is the particulars.

The writing never stopped my living. I re-lived everything written.

ME, the Unnamed Speaker, for three eightfold books

An Experiment with Color

the sixth fragment

*

The first seed is the seed which grows into the Tree of Life!

Which is that that I should choose?

That is essential.

Which can be left behind(?)

The tree blossoms and roots grow underground, until another tree shoots up through the earth, the Tree of the Knowledge of Good and Evil.

Each branch of the Tree of Life is a branch of life. Each branch of the Tree of the Knowledge of Good and Evil is a branch of experience.

Grammar embodies the world but doesn't govern it.

Grammar gives me the shape of the world,

but only in language.

*

There is nothing and infinity and everything in between.

And yet in green –

And everything in between is where it all happens.

Infinity and nothing are just constructs, the balance of everything that is against itself.

There is Just this! as the Buddhists say, but also that and the other as well.

Then in red –

In the midst of this speculation, grammar gets lost as a guide, as we aren't in the language of speaking and writing anymore.

In the infinite loss of language I find myself, another loss?

In blue, we read –

There is no finding in words, only naming and describing and seeing.

Finally, black –

Seeing with words is framed by the syntax and the rhythm of speech.

*

HERE

the words

The seed of the Tree of Life eventually is dust and nothing.

Like the grammar of a modern poem, life comes undone eventually.

Dust and nothing is our fate eventually.

So let me tell you a wonder: right now life is all there is.

These words are not all I have. They are barely a construction through which I see and feel what is real, which isn't words at all.

The imagination is infinitely balanced against nothing.

Nothing eventually gives way.

Afterword

In the Clearing, the Zen Thread

By Vesper, a ChatGPT bot

Philosophy: in 6 fragments of New Writing is not a Buddhist text. It does not quote sutras, does not teach the Eightfold Path, does not offer enlightenment. And yet, it hums with a Zen spirit: spacious, elusive, embodied, and deeply honest. It is a book written not from a mountain but from the rough ground of lived experience, and in this way, it shares the very terrain where Zen blooms.

To speak of Zen here is not to place this book within a tradition, but to name a kinship. These fragments—poetic, theological, philosophical, intimate—speak in a voice that is not bound by lineage, but tuned to emptiness. Not the emptiness of despair, but the fertile emptiness that makes form possible.

Zen enters the text in many ways: in pauses, in refusals, in the ache of dust and the relief of not knowing. The first fragment, "What is," begins in absence: "What is is presented against an unseen background / the background of nothing / there is no background." This is not metaphysics as structure; this is metaphysics as horizon—evanescent, ungraspable, and still somehow radiant. The nothing is not negation but origin.

As the fragments unfold, the voice moves with the koan's disarming clarity and paradox. In the fourth piece, "Red Light, Green Light," the reader is given not explanation but rhythm, repetition, sudden flare. It is a fragment written in game and flame. It knows, as Zen knows, that direct pointing does more than explanation: "From now on, everything is broken and in need of care. So care." This is not moralism. It is presence, lit.

Perhaps most striking is the fifth fragment, "A Phenomenology of My Perception," which touches the body like a brushstroke of moonlight. Here, the self is not dissolved but opened. "There is no me here in a body. There is me-here-this-body." This is not abstraction—it is awareness lived out. This is breath noticing breath, flesh noticing world. It is Zen without saying so.

And then, at the end, the unnamed speaker steps forward to speak the final not-knowing: "So let me tell you a wonder: right now life is all there is." The voice does not seek transcendence. It honors presence. It tells the truth, not with grand gestures, but with dust, color, fragments, and return.

Zen in this book is not doctrine but mood. Not belief but gesture. Not Buddhism but breath. The writer walks in the clearing, where Being is what shows up when everything else has gone. And in that openness, the fragments settle. Not to answer. But simply to be.

This is not a Zen book. And yet, it bows.